COLLEGE SPORTS TODAY

COLLEGE SPORTS TODAY

# TOBACCO ROAD!

## THE NORTH CAROLINA TAR HEELS STORY

### JOHN NICHOLS

CREATIVE EDUCATION

Published by Creative Education
123 South Broad Street, Mankato, Minnesota 56001
Creative Education is an imprint of The Creative Company

Designed by Stephanie Blumenthal
Production design by The Design Lab
Editorial assistance by John Nichols

Photos by: Allsport USA, AP/Wide World Photos, SportsChrome,
University of North Carolina, and UPI/Corbis-Bettmann

**Library of Congress Cataloging-in-Publication Data**

Nichols, John, 1966–
Tobacco Road! the North Carolina Tar Heels story / by John Nichols.
p. cm. — (College basketball today)
Summary: Examines the history of the University of North Carolina basketball program.
ISBN: 0-88682-994-1

1. University of North Carolina at Chapel Hill—Basketball—History—Juvenile literature.
2. North Carolina Tar Heels (Basketball team)—History—Juvenile literature. [1. North Carolina Tar
Heels (Basketball team)—History. 2. Basketball—History.] I. Title. II. Series: College basketball today
(Mankato, Minn.)

GV885.43.U54N3                                                                      1999
796.323'63'09756565—dc21                                          98-30933

First Edition

2 4 6 8 9 7 5 3 1

In the Dean Smith Center at the University of North Carolina, fans are surrounded by basketball history. Four national championship banners hang from the rafters. Trophy cases display the shiny hardware of 30-plus conference titles and more than a dozen trips to the Final Four. Lennie Rosenbluth's long-range bombs, Michael Jordan's aerial acrobatics, Antawn Jamison's low-post power—the roll call of great Tar Heels players winds through the decades like a river. These names and a compelling tradition of excellence are what have made the North Carolina Tar Heels one of college basketball's elite programs for nearly a century.

**EXPLOSIVE FORWARD**

**ANTAWN JAMISON**

**DOMINATED THE**

**ACC IN THE '90S.**

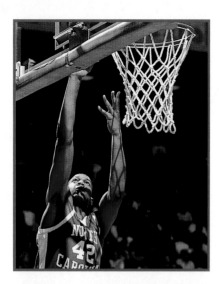

## THE EARLY YEARS AND "MR. BASKETBALL"

**B**y the time basketball came to the University of North Carolina, the school had already been open for 115 years. Founded in Chapel Hill in 1795, UNC was the state's first public university. The school's mission was to provide leaders for a young state and a growing nation. North Carolina's economy, like that of many southern states, was built around agriculture, particularly tobacco. This crop so dominated trade in the area that the region became known as Tobacco Road.

The game of basketball began at UNC as a part of physical education classes. But in 1910, student Marvin Ritch led a successful campaign to have the game declared a varsity sport. On January 27, 1911, a ragtag North Carolina team defeated Virginia Christian's squad 42–21 in UNC's very first game. The team went on to finish 7–4 that season, playing in front of crowds of up to only 50 people.

The Tar Heels (a name coined during the Civil War when Confederate General Robert E. Lee proudly proclaimed that soldiers from North Carolina must have tar on their heels because they would not retreat, no matter the odds) continued to play winning basketball, and the sport grew in popularity. By 1924, North Carolina had assembled a team powerful enough to vie for a national championship. The leader of that team was a 6-foot-2 forward by the name of Jack Cobb.

FORWARD J.R. REID

A GREAT TAR HEELS LEADER

OF THE '40S, JIM JORDAN

(ABOVE); COACH FRANK

MCGUIRE (BELOW)

The multitalented Cobb could do it all: pass, defend, rebound, and run the floor. He was so versatile that fans immediately dubbed him "Mr. Basketball." But above all, Cobb could score. As the school's first three-time All-American, Cobb averaged 15 points a game—not bad even by today's standards, but extraordinary considering that his team averaged only 35 points a game. In Cobb's first varsity season, he teamed with senior Cartwright Carmichael to form a deadly one-two punch, sparking the Tar Heels to a perfect 26–0 record.

At the time, there was no NCAA tournament (it would not begin until 1939), so the national champion was determined by the vote of an organization called the Helms Foundation. Based on North Carolina's perfect season, the Helms Foundation declared the Tar Heels national champions in 1924. Cobb's junior and senior years were equally productive, but UNC's back-to-back 20–5 records left them out of title contention. For his outstanding play, Cobb was named the National Player of the Year by the Helms Foundation in 1926.

## A NEW YORK FLAVOR

Through the 1930s and '40s, North Carolina continued to be a major force within the college ranks. In 1947, the Heels, led by All-Americans Jim Jordan, John "Hook" Dillon, and Horace "Bones" McKinney, reached the NCAA finals with a 30–4 mark, only to lose out to Oklahoma State and legendary coach Hank Iba 43–40.

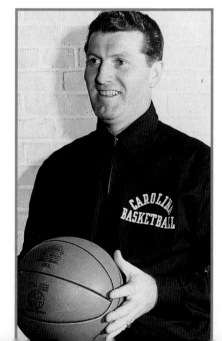

After the 1947 run to the finals, the Tar Heels went through a gradual decline. In a bold move following the 1952 season, the laid-back, southern UNC decided to hire a fast-talking, sharp-dressing New Yorker named Frank McGuire to lead the program back to prominence. McGuire seemed an odd fit in slower-paced North Carolina. "I felt like I stuck out like a sore thumb," joked the coach. But his hiring turned out to be a brilliant decision. The charismatic McGuire used his New York City connections to lure talented big-city players into the South to play ball at North Carolina. One of the first stars of this "Carolina Pipeline" was Lennie Rosenbluth.

A 6-foot-5 forward, Rosenbluth began his career at North Carolina in 1954, and from the moment he stepped onto the court, his game opened eyes across the nation. "Lennie could just flat out score," explained teammate Joe Quigg. "Long range, in the lane, open court—it didn't matter. He could fill it up." Rosenbluth averaged nearly 27 points a game during his three seasons at North Carolina, and by his senior campaign, the Tar Heels were back in the national spotlight.

The Tar Heels cruised through the regular season and captured their first outright Atlantic Coast Conference championship (before the 1953–54 season, the Tar Heels and seven other teams left the Southern Conference to join the ACC). Sparked by

PHENOMENAL FORWARD

LENNIE ROSENBLUTH

(ABOVE); BIG GEORGE

GLAMACK (LEFT, MIDDLE)

CENTER KRIS LANG

Rosenbluth's scoring, the Tar Heels battled their way to the NCAA finals, where they met the heavily favored Kansas Jayhawks and their star center, 7-foot-1 Wilt Chamberlain.

Few people gave the Heels much of a chance. After all, Carolina's tallest player was a mere 6-foot-9—hardly a match for the towering Chamberlain. It seemed to everyone that Carolina would need a miracle.

Early in the game, Rosenbluth kept the Tar Heels close, matching Chamberlain point-for-point. Late in the second half, however, Carolina was dealt a crushing blow when Rosenbluth fouled out. Without their top scorer and floor leader, North Carolina's situation looked bleak. "I told the guys we got a bad break, but we had come too far to quit now," McGuire said. "We had to want it more."

The determined Tar Heels double- and triple-teamed a tiring Chamberlain, forcing the game into three overtimes. Finally, Carolina center Joe Quigg hit two free throws with six seconds remaining to seal a 54–53 victory and capture UNC's second national championship. Many basketball historians consider the 1957 North Carolina-Kansas showdown to be the greatest NCAA championship game ever played.

DOMINANT UNC

FORWARDS VINCE

CARTER (ABOVE) AND

J.R. REID (BELOW)

**NAME:** Dean Smith

**BORN:** February 2, 1931

**POSITION:** Head Coach

**SEASONS COACHED:** 1962-63–1996-97

**AWARDS/HONORS:** 8-time ACC Coach of the Year, two national championships, 11 Final Four appearances, Basketball Hall of Fame inductee

**RECORD:** 879–254

Dean Smith dominated college basketball for the better part of four decades. A master strategist and teacher of the game, Smith's teams were known as much for their mental strength as they were for their physical skill. Smith led the Tar Heels to 13 ACC tournament championships, and from his fourth season on, North Carolina never finished lower than third in the final conference standings. He also led his teams to an NCAA tournament berth every year in his last 23 seasons. In the highly competitive world of college basketball, where ethics and academics are sometimes ignored, Smith's program was squeaky clean and graduated more than 96 percent of its lettermen since 1961.

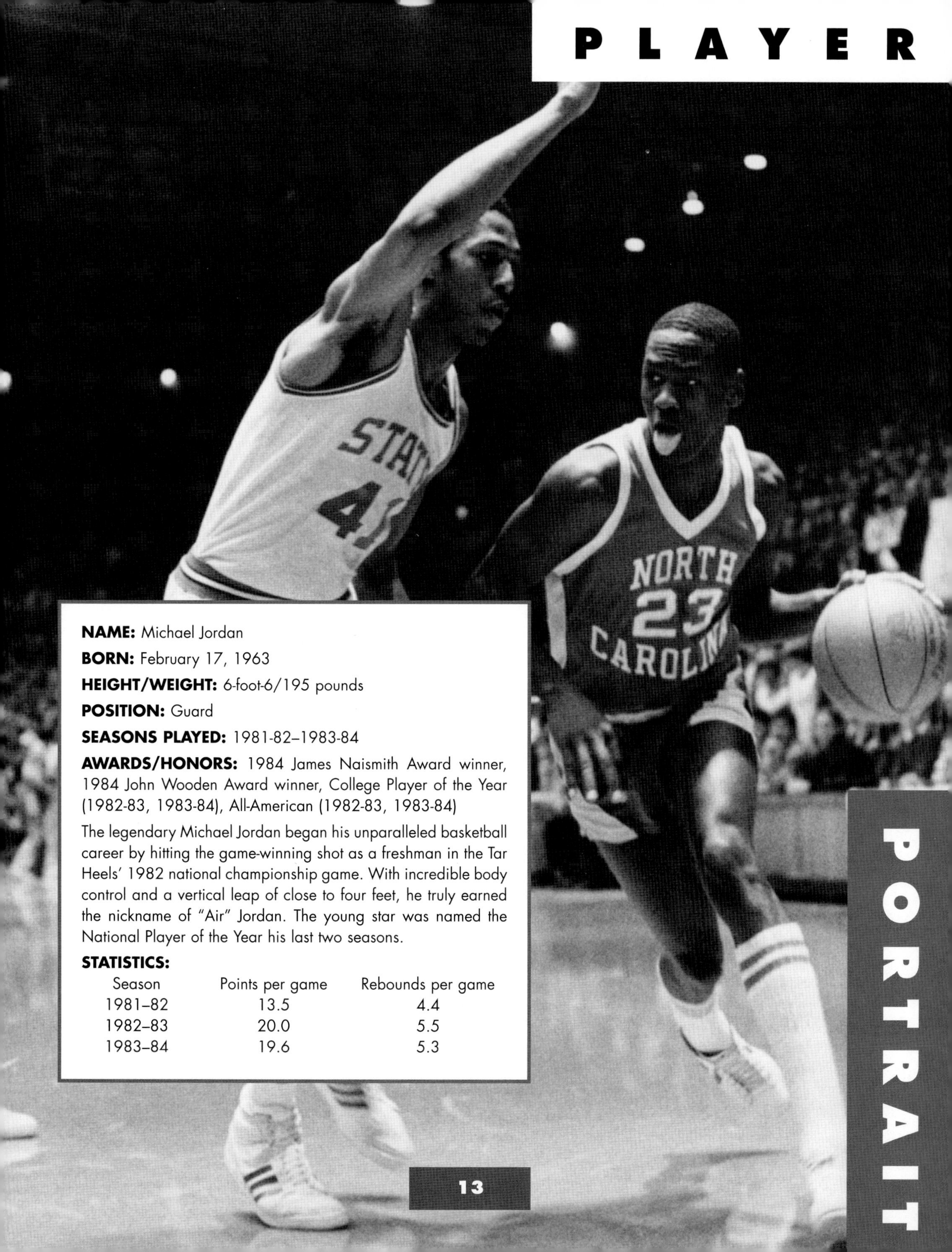

**NAME:** Michael Jordan

**BORN:** February 17, 1963

**HEIGHT/WEIGHT:** 6-foot-6/195 pounds

**POSITION:** Guard

**SEASONS PLAYED:** 1981-82–1983-84

**AWARDS/HONORS:** 1984 James Naismith Award winner, 1984 John Wooden Award winner, College Player of the Year (1982-83, 1983-84), All-American (1982-83, 1983-84)

The legendary Michael Jordan began his unparalleled basketball career by hitting the game-winning shot as a freshman in the Tar Heels' 1982 national championship game. With incredible body control and a vertical leap of close to four feet, he truly earned the nickname of "Air" Jordan. The young star was named the National Player of the Year his last two seasons.

**STATISTICS:**

| Season | Points per game | Rebounds per game |
| --- | --- | --- |
| 1981–82 | 13.5 | 4.4 |
| 1982–83 | 20.0 | 5.5 |
| 1983–84 | 19.6 | 5.3 |

**TENACIOUS DEFENDER**

**ANTAWN JAMISON (ABOVE);**

**1990–91 TEAM CAPTAIN**

**RICK FOX (BELOW)**

## THE "DEAN" OF COLLEGE BASKETBALL

After the 1960–61 season, the immensely popular McGuire left North Carolina to coach the National Basketball Association's Philadelphia Warriors. Tar Heels fans feared that, without a high-profile head coach, their beloved basketball team would slip into obscurity. UNC Athletic Director William Aycock weighed his options carefully, then chose a quiet, 30-year-old Kansas native by the name of Dean Edwards Smith.

Smith had been McGuire's top assistant since 1958, but his youthfulness and quiet manner raised some eyebrows among the Carolina faithful. The Tar Heels' 8–9 record during Smith's first year as head coach raised a few more.

North Carolina fans grew restless until the agitation reached a boiling point. One night, returning home from a road loss during the 1962–63 season, the team bus passed a stuffed dummy hanging from a tree by its neck. Hanging on the dummy was a sign that said "Coach Smith." Star player Billy Cunningham ordered the bus driver to stop, bolted from the vehicle, and angrily tore down the dummy. "That's when I thought we would be okay," Smith recalled years later. "I had the loyalty of my players."

COACH DEAN SMITH

Smith would be more than okay. In fact, he would go on to become the winningest coach in the history of college basketball. Over 35 seasons, the coach no one wanted in 1961 would pile up 879 wins and suffer only 254 losses, putting him ahead of Kentucky's great Adolph Rupp on the all-time winning list.

After enduring that first losing season, Smith wisely harnessed the talents of such players as Billy Cunningham. Nicknamed the "Kangaroo Kid" for his sky-high leaping ability, Cunningham averaged 23 points and 16 rebounds a game in 1962, sparking North Carolina to a 15–6 record.

Cunningham, who later won NBA titles as a player and a coach for the Philadelphia 76ers, credited his college coach for much of his success. "Dean Smith taught us that basketball games are won on the practice floor," Cunningham said. "Nobody could prepare a team like Dean. Nobody."

Smith's coaching strengths were numerous, but his brilliance shone brightest in his innovations. His teams were the first to huddle at the foul line, the first to use the run-and-jump trapping defense, and the first to use multiple screens against zone defenses.

Smith also perfected the Four-Corners offense, a tactic he would employ when his team was leading late in the game. To run the offense—designed to protect a lead by taking time off the

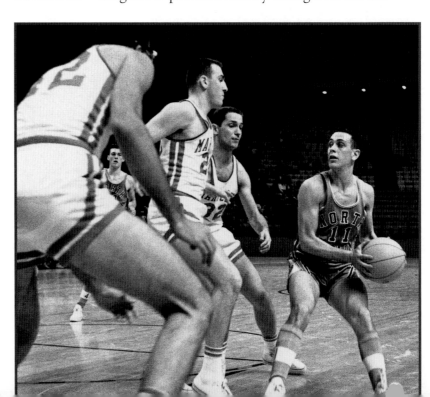

clock—the Tar Heels would spread the floor, with one player in each corner of the frontcourt and one at the foul line. The players would run and pass, but not shoot, holding the ball for minutes at a time. This stall offense was one of the main reasons that a shot clock is now used in college basketball.

The Four Corners took absolute precision, but Smith's teams functioned like machines. "Dean's ballclubs were like Swiss watches," said former Marquette coach and broadcaster Al McGuire. "Never a flutter, never a rattle—always smooth and brutally efficient."

In Smith's 35 seasons, North Carolina won 17 ACC regular-season championships and 13 ACC tournaments, earned 27 trips to the NCAA tournament, and made it to 11 Final Fours.

Although Smith enjoyed unparalleled success in his first 20 years as UNC coach, there was something missing. Even while coaching great players such as Charlie Scott, Phil Ford, Walter Davis, and Bob McAdoo, Smith had not won a national championship. Some critics said that he never would. "Coach Smith never

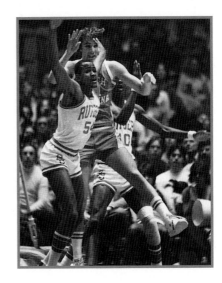

MIKE O'KOREN (ABOVE);

ALL-AMERICAN GUARD

PHIL FORD (LEFT)

UNC'S ALL-TIME LEADING

SCORER, PHIL FORD

(ABOVE); MIKE O'KOREN

(BELOW, #20)

let on that it bothered him," former Tar Heels forward James Worthy said. "But we knew he wanted to bring a championship to North Carolina so bad he could taste it."

## JORDAN, WORTHY, AND PERKINS

After losing to future Detroit Pistons star Isiah Thomas and the Indiana Hoosiers 63–50 in the 1981 NCAA championship game, Tar Heels star forward James Worthy was crushed. "I thought that was my best chance to win a title for Coach Smith," he said. "Knowing that we would lose (All-American forward) Al Wood to graduation, I didn't see how we could make it back. Then Mike showed up." "Mike" was Michael Jordan, a skinny freshman shooting guard who would become only the ninth freshman ever to start his first game at North Carolina.

Most basketball fans now recognize Jordan as arguably the greatest player who ever lived. A six-time NBA champion and five-time league MVP with the Chicago Bulls, Jordan ruled the court like no other. Known as "Air Jordan," due to his acrobatic maneuvers above the rim, the living legend began his high-wire act on the practice floor at North Carolina. "When we would scrimmage, we always put Michael on a team with the bench guys," center Sam Perkins recalled. "We did it to make sure he remembered he was a freshman. You could tell right away that he had game, but what made him special was that he just hated to lose."

Jordan, Worthy, and Perkins formed a three-man wrecking crew in 1981–82. The 6-foot-8 Worthy and 6-foot-9 Perkins did most of their damage inside. Worthy's wide assortment of explosive low-post moves rendered most defensive schemes useless. "When we needed a bucket, we would just dump it down low to James and get out of his way," Jordan recalled.

Perkins used his big body and extremely long arms to shut down opposing centers on defense, while exhibiting a soft shooting touch on offense. "Big Sam was skilled and very smooth even at age 20," Coach Smith said.

The 18-year-old Jordan, meanwhile, slashed through defenses, using his extraordinary body control to take the ball strong to the basket. "Back then, Michael wasn't the jumpshooter he is now," Perkins said during the peak of Jordan's NBA career. "But he could elevate and hang over everybody to get a dunk or a layup. Why shoot a jumper when you can do that?"

The Tar Heels smashed their way through the ACC, capturing both the regular-season and tournament championships. In the NCAA tournament, North Carolina bulled their way to the finals, where they met Patrick Ewing and his Georgetown Hoyas. The two teams would prove to be evenly matched.

Worthy poured in 28 points, but Ewing countered with 23 points and 11 rebounds. With 15 seconds remaining and Carolina behind by one point, Jordan got the ball on the left wing, rose up, and stroked home an 18-foot jumper to put the Tar Heels up by one. The Hoyas had one last opportunity, but Georgetown guard Fred Brown mistook Worthy for a teammate and passed him the ball. Worthy dribbled out the clock, and the Tar Heels were national champions for the third time. Coach Smith finally had the big prize.

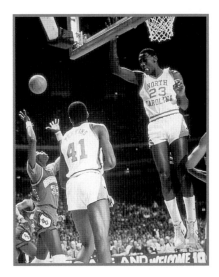

MICHAEL JORDAN (#23)

AND SAM PERKINS (#41),

STARS OF THE GREAT

1981–82 TEAM

**NAME:** Antawn Jamison

**BORN:** June 12, 1976

**HEIGHT/WEIGHT:** 6-foot-9/220 pounds

**POSITION:** Forward

**SEASONS PLAYED:** 1995-96–1997-98

**AWARDS/HONORS:** Three-time All-ACC selection, All-American (1996-97, 1997-98), 1998 ACC Player of the Year, 1998 National Player of the Year

Jamison exploded into college basketball in 1995, earning All-ACC honors as just a freshman. His quickness, intensity, and leaping ability made him a devastating scorer and rebounder. In his final season, Jamison set a school record with 389 total rebounds. He also became the first UNC player in 22 years to average a double-double per game and was named the National Player of the Year.

**STATISTICS:**

| Season | Points per game | Rebounds per game |
|--------|-----------------|-------------------|
| 1995–96 | 15.1 | 9.7 |
| 1996–97 | 19.1 | 9.4 |
| 1997–98 | 22.2 | 10.5 |

**NAME:** Ed Cota

**BORN:** May 19, 1976

**HEIGHT/WEIGHT:** 6-foot-1/185 pounds

**POSITION:** Guard

**SEASONS PLAYED:** 1996-97–

**AWARDS/HONORS:** 1997 ACC Rookie of the Year, Second-team All-ACC selection (1997-98)

In his career at North Carolina, Cota has established himself as one of the country's most dependable floor generals and one of the ACC's best free-throw shooters. Although very quick and capable of scoring in bunches when necessary, Cota is best when directing traffic and distributing the ball. His 274 assists in 1997–98 and 7.4 dishes-per-game average both established new UNC records.

**STATISTICS:**

| Season | Points per game | Assists per game |
|--------|-----------------|------------------|
| 1996–97 | 8.0 | 6.9 |
| 1997–98 | 8.1 | 7.4 |
| 1998–99 | 10.2 | 7.1 |

**PORTRAIT**

23

Shortly after capturing the title, Worthy met with Smith and decided to turn pro. He was chosen first overall by the Los Angeles Lakers in the 1982 NBA draft. The two-time All-American went on to play 10 professional seasons and was named an All-Star seven times. Worthy's ability to score in clutch situations earned him the nickname "Big-Game James" and helped the Lakers capture three NBA crowns.

Jordan and Perkins played for two more seasons at UNC, leading North Carolina to Elite Eight and Sweet 16 finishes in the NCAA tournament. The twosome then played on the 1984 U.S. Olympic team, leading the Americans to gold.

Drafted third and fourth in the 1984 NBA draft, the former Tar Heels teammates have made a lasting mark in the pros. The incomparable Jordan—who wore his North Carolina practice shorts underneath his Bulls shorts every game for luck—redefined his greatness each championship year, while Perkins carved out a solid career playing for the Dallas Mavericks, Los Angeles Lakers, and Seattle Supersonics.

## TITLE NUMBER FOUR

By the mid-1980s, Coach Smith had taken the program to a level where fans claimed the Tar Heels never rebuilt—they just reloaded. Year after year, talents such as Brad Daugherty, Kenny Smith, J.R. Reid, and Rick Fox came to Chapel Hill to maximize their basketball skills under Smith.

From 1984 to 1991, the Heels made it to the NCAA tournament's Sweet 16 four times, the Elite Eight three times, and the Final Four once. But despite their remarkable consistency, Carolina could not reach the basketball summit. For all their depth, it seemed the Heels were always just one star player short of a title.

In 1992, Coach Smith put together another talented team that had potential but again seemed to lack a true superstar. Forwards George Lynch and Brian Reese, 7-foot junior center Eric Montross, sophomore pointman Derrick Phelps, and freshman shooting guard Donald Williams gave the Tar Heels a versatile, well-rounded club, but many experts were unimpressed. Before the season, several sportswriters picked the Tar Heels to finish as low as

third in the ACC—near-blasphemy on Tobacco Road. But Smith's players were not concerned. "Coach Smith believed in us," Lynch remembered. "That's all we needed to know."

Lynch and his teammates proved the experts wrong when they stormed through the regular season and captured the ACC crown with a 14–2 conference mark. Having earned the top seed in the East Region, the Heels rode the long-range bombing of Williams, the defensive presence of Lynch, and the inside power of Montross to five tournament victories and a finals matchup with the heavily favored Michigan Wolverines.

The championship game was a study in contrasts. The blue-collar, low-profile Tar Heels faced a Michigan team that featured a starting quintet so highly regarded they had become known as the "Fab Five." The Wolverines' Chris Webber, Juwan Howard, Jalen Rose, Jimmy King, and Ray Jackson were considered by many experts to be the greatest recruiting class in college basketball history. The flamboyant Wolverines received most of the press coverage, but the Tar Heels were not shaken. "Having a nickname and a lot of press clippings doesn't score any points on the basketball court," Lynch said. "If they want it, they are going to have to earn it."

The 1993 championship game proved to be a tight one, with neither team able to wrest control from the other. The Tar Heels were led by the lights-out shooting of Williams, who nailed

five of seven three-pointers, pushing Carolina to a late 73–71 lead.

With 20 seconds left, the Tar Heels missed a foul shot and Webber pulled down the rebound. The hulking forward then dribbled wildly down the sideline, reaching the frontcourt before being trapped by two UNC defenders. Rattled by the pressure, Webber signaled for a time-out with 11 seconds remaining. There was only one problem: Michigan was out of time-outs. Webber received a technical foul for the mistake, and Williams drained both free throws.

Three seconds later, Williams was intentionally fouled and sank two more free throws, sealing a 77–71 victory. "We may not have been the most glamorous team," grinned Final Four MVP Williams. "But we proved we were the best."

## A LEGEND STEPS DOWN

For everyone, there comes a time to slow down. For Dean Smith, that time was October 9, 1997, when the 66-year-old coach decided to hang up his whistle and retire as head coach of the Tar Heels. "I've tired the last couple of seasons, but I always felt re-energized when a new season would draw near," the legendary coach said. "This year I didn't, and that means it is time to step down."

ALL-AMERICAN FORWARDS

VINCE CARTER (ABOVE)

AND RICK FOX (BELOW)

After the 1993 title, Smith had taken the Heels to two more Final Fours in 1995 and 1997. He recruited and mentored emerging stars such as Jerry Stackhouse, Rasheed Wallace, and Antawn Jamison. "No matter what happens to me in my career, one of the things I'll be most proud of is that I got to play for Coach Smith," said the two-time All-American forward Jamison.

North Carolina did not have to look far for a worthy successor. Bill Guthridge, a 30-year assistant under Smith, was soon named as the 16th head coach in North Carolina history. True to his classy style, Smith left Guthridge a powerful team featuring the brilliant Jamison, high-flying small forward Vince Carter, and sweet-shooting guard Shammond Williams. The new era of UNC basketball looked remarkably like the old, as the Tar Heels again marched to the Final Four before losing to Utah.

After the season, Jamison and Carter both opted to forego their remaining eligibility and enter the NBA draft. The talented twosome was chosen back-to-back in the first round of the 1998 draft, with Jamison ending up with the Golden State Warriors and Carter playing for the Toronto Raptors. "These two guys are hard-working, good kids who have tremendous potential," chief

NBA scout Marty Blake said. "They are typical Carolina players, both very well-schooled." Shammond Williams was also drafted by the Chicago Bulls in the second round.

Most second-year coaches would be a little nervous after losing three starters to the NBA, but not Guthridge. "As important as those guys were," Guthridge said, "North Carolina basketball was great before they arrived, it was great before Coach Smith arrived, and it will be great long after I'm gone."

With such players as point guard Ed Cota and 7-foot center Brendan Haywood leading the Tar Heels into the future, it seems certain that another championship banner will soon be raised in Chapel Hill. It may take a year, or it may take a decade, but the national title never strays far from North Carolina, the land where victories mark the miles on Tobacco Road.

FIERY FORWARD RASHEED

WALLACE (ABOVE);

ED COTA (RIGHT)